THE ETHICS OF CATS

Alice Kinsella is an Arts Council of Ireland Next Generation Artist. *The Ethics of Cats* is her first full-length poetry collection. She lives in Co. Mayo with her family.

Also by Alice Kinsella

Wake of the Whale (Mayo Books, 2024)

Milk: On Motherhood and Madness (Picador, 2023)

Sexy Fruit (Broken Sleep Books, 2018)

Flower Press (Onslaught, 2018)

CONTENTS

CIRQUE DU SOLEIL CAT   11

I. NEBULA

CHOOSE YOUR OWN ADVENTURE PARALYSIS   15

PILGRIMAGE   17

EXISTENTIAL CRISIS AS APOCALYPSE   25

SEX ED. 2004   26

D.O.S.E   27

LEAVING HOME (AGAIN)   28

EXISTENTIAL CRISIS AS ADDICTION   29

GIRL   30

BIRTHDAY   31

ECLIPSING BLOOD MOON   33

CHASING FRUIT FLIES AROUND THE HOUSE   34

STARTING FIRES   36

THE DOCTOR (WHO?) WAS A WOMAN   37

CHARLOTTE PERKINS-GILMAN   38

NEBULA (OR, PREMONITION)   40

II. BIG HOUSE

CHARACTER DEVELOPMENT   43

A HISTORY OF MENTAL HEALTH CARE IN FIVE ACTS   47

CARE/COMMUNITY   58

III. THE ETHICS OF CATS

(RE)WILD	65
THE WALKOUT	66
I DIDN'T NAME YOU FOR A KING	68
PULLING BACK THE DRAPES ON A DECEMBER MORNING	71
IN THE BELLY	72
NEUTRALITY	74
IN THE NAME OF	76
THE KITTEN IS IN HEAT	77
CRESCENDO	78
PLAYING HOUSE	79
TWO MAMS TALKING	81
THE CAT KILLS A MOUSE	82
EVOLUTION	83
YES, AND BACK AGAIN	86
CODE-SWITCHING	88
FAT CATS	89
HOT CAT DAD	90
ZIGGY	91
IN THE BELLY (CONT.)	93
EXISTENTIAL CRISIS AS ANTHROPOCENE	94
IN THE PISSINGS OF RAIN IN KINVARA	95
WHISTLE	96
ROADKILL: A DRAMA	98
PALE BLUE DOT	101
NOTES	102
ACKNOWLEDGMENTS	105

For E, my love, always and forever.

*For Dan, without whom there would be no poetry
and I would be no poet.*

*And for Ickyblicky, Sunshine, Penguin, Mitten, Moses, Charlie,
Pixie, Goblin, Sugar, Monkey, Button, Cookie, Monster, Ellie,
Moose, Tallullah, Tilly, Millie, Roanie, Lola, Lilith, and Ziggy.
Suppose I can't use your names as passwords now.*

© 2025, Alice Kinsella. All rights reserved; no part of this book may be reproduced by any means without the publisher's permission.

ISBN: 978-1-917617-12-3

The author has asserted their right to be identified as the author of this Work in accordance with the Copyright, Designs and Patents Act 1988

Cover designed by Aaron Kent

Typeset by Aaron Kent

Broken Sleep Books Ltd
PO BOX 102
Llandysul
SA44 9BG

The Ethics of Cats

Alice Kinsella

Broken Sleep Books

What is love?
Oh baby, don't hurt me
  — Haddaway

The cats at civil war
in the partition garden.
I stroke my whiskers.
   — Michael Hartnett

CIRQUE DU SOLEIL CAT

My cat tosses a pygmy shrew in the air
like a pancake. Stiff little legs stick straight up.
Had I kept all her doorstep-deposited gifts
I'd have a glove by now, impossibly soft.
Or a coat, accounting for two decades
of cats' butchery: Cruella worthy,
floor sweeping. She throws the corpse
from one paw to the other, a juggler,
Cirque du Soleil cat. She's having a brilliant time.

*

Beyond the school bus window,
morning dark glowed with eyes,
shiny as millennium punts.
Not the cat's eyes that illuminate
significant routes, but leverets
by the dozen, darting from the headlights.
In second year, a mink-farm jailbreak
—rumour had it, an inside job—
extinguished the reflectors.

That spring, I tried to stab
a sixth-year lad
with my tech-graphics compass.
Word was he'd bitten the head
off a live chicken.

*

Mum didn't kill spiders.
She threw them out the window,
'til I pointed out spiders can't fly.

*

My cats worked together.
Grown kittens took down a hare,
their mother enveloped its head with her jaw.

*

Hares ruin the bark of young trees.
I feed my cat dehydrated chicken guts.
Shrews dine on eight-legged victims of gravity.
My diet is vegetarian, mainly eggs and cheese.
How far does empathy reach?

*

The cat chucks the shrew above her head,
snaps it from the air mid-fall, spits it out,
like a baby rejecting mushed carrot.
She is bored of the dead.
A butterfly goes by, she chases it.

I. Nebula

Human madness is oftentimes a cunning and most feline thing.
— Hermann Melville

Love is like a brick. You can build a house, or you can sink a dead body.
— Lady Gaga

CHOOSE YOUR OWN ADVENTURE PARALYSIS

I've been writing an alternative history book
in my head. One where all the same wars happened
only I travelled by train across Europe like I meant to,

and lost weight and wore denim shorts and had hair
like Alanis Morrissette and did learn to speak Irish
and lived on the Aran islands and didn't fall in love
(at least not so young and so frequently).

Every cigarette is doing me damage, so I quit and dwell
instead on The Paris Agreement and single car crashes.

I'm trying to relive my youth
before it's over. It's legal to fuck someone born
in this millennium. Being young (if I remember
correctly) has been:

> Eyesight good enough to see hair I was too lazy to pluck.
>
> Calling Home Ec. a tool of patriarchal depression then
> needing to google *how to mop a floor* at 22.
>
> Ignoring cystitis to avoid antibiotics (you can't drink
> on antibiotics), then ending up in A&E with a kidney
> infection.

I thought life would look different by now.

8 or 9 and I'm drawing a horse.
It doesn't look like I'd meant it to look.
It's flat (I have no perspective) I cry.
Can't change it, can't force it, or go back
and correct, correct correct it.

I'm worried I've been making the wrong mistakes.

PILGRIMAGE

Haworth

The first visit, years gone, hit with a wallop of words.
I arrived in some kind of heart's home.
Now, despite synchrony, stars won't align.

I buy a brochure from the blue corner shop
pushing Brontë merch, English pubs, and the ascent—
that climb to Emily's quarry of emotional excess

from which she carved her indelible structure.
Now bless me, I'm having what you might call a crisis
of faith. But what prayers exist for the faithless?

I find a signed first edition of *Station Island,*
five pounds, not re-priced since Heaney's death.
It must be a sign,

laughs the bookseller,
with phantasmal Yorkshire wit.
I think, maybe an omen

for this Irish girl,
neglecting heritage
before drowning in it.

Brontë Waterfall with Grouse

Off the track towards the birth
   of water bubbling over from the earth,

heather and ferns hold out their hands
   pull me to this hideaway, where blocks of sand-

stone balance like steps from a faraway Eden.
   The stream filters rust like glitter. I am bleeding

again, I can feel the cleaving, the rush in my groin.
   Wet shale gleams like fountain coins.

The flow lulls but berates, dashing its weight
   on rocks waiting for destruction. It's getting late,

I've lost sight of the peak, the house's silhouette, my goal.
   I wash my hands and face, leave my shoes on, it's cold

for September and the moor is not kind.
   Sit with the symphony of the fall: *rest / you're falling behind.*

It's the red that I spot, like stained underthings
   eclipsing a dress, the crown he wears even in death. Wings

bent like broken bones, wet as new kittens. Claws
   closed on air, bead eye forced to stare, beak open mid-pause.

I want to pet the oil slick of his neck, close his eye, beg he
  forgive my disrupting his decay with my need for epiphany

I can't find in poems. I tell him I'm after what I've lost at home:
  some kind of jumpstart, a shock to the heart. Might I find it alone

on the moor? Which must hold a power, answer to the mystery.
  The water aids his dissolution. I can see

how unforgiving nature can be, yet there's a blood-deep shake
  and for the briefest of seconds do I glimpse the sublime?

The flow shifts, the light dips, the clouds threaten to break.
  I continue to climb.

Ascent

This peace is outrageous. Something must fill it.
Chuckles of grouse, the odd hysterical pheasant.
Far-off, a rock falls. Here, the air jolts. Rushes bend
and quiver, waves roll over them. Wind, my breath,
my heartbeat. This is where people bring their grief.

There's a suggestion
of garden, lawn shorn by sheep
teeth, stones pop their heads
from the grass to say *wall*.

I read Sylvia Plath's *Wuthering Heights*
on my phone.

Two Sycamore trees,
black-spotted leaves, crumpled
like bat wings, fret on branch ends.
The crunch of the first falls this year.
Against the roots of one tree: a yellow rose,
wrapped in plastic which will outlast
the standing of these stones.

Dawn Chorus for the Dead
They rest until the day breaks
And the shadows flee away

The rooks wake before day breaks
and deliver me their caws
through the canopy
cloaking Haworth cemetery

parsonage windows dark
        could be sleeping
church locked overnight
        could be sleeping

        slip of cobbles under foot
clip clop clip clop
        Victorian light black mist
        streetlamps like fires
        catlike I slip through shadows
tip tap slap slap
        of my footfalls
close distance

chaos peaceful in the absence
of all earthbound heartbeats
other than my own so tightly
held beneath my tongue

the bells ring welcoming
seven Sunday morning

bing bong bong bing
all houses snooze still
rooks scream their panic
crescendo crescendo!

Until the shadows break
And the day flees away
They rest

The Haunting of Sylvia Plath

I have no faith,
but the world keeps
handing me miracles.

Misty day halfway to heavens. So close
this whole time. Heptonstall sleeps like a ghost town.
No cars crushing cobbles, no chit-chat on the street.
Could be a film set or a dream. No signs, no plaque,
no Sylvia mugs in the shops. Her tragedy too new,
a modern myth. Give it a hundred years, persevere.

The churchyard is committed to wildness.
Medieval bones of prayer withstand the briars
that rise up like waves to engulf them.

At the gate, yellow poppies big as fists
welcome me. Bees bob in and out.
The sun, high and bright, holds no heat,
white as starlight. I have no map.
Instinct guides me. Still as the photographs.
I don't have to queue for an audience.
It baffles me to my knees.

Her earth overgrown with foxgloves, weeds,
crumpled bouquets, pens, lipsticks, stones.
This impossible stillness. This quiet.

I have no prayer. What use is poetry here?
I garden, pull up the weeds that choke
the flowers, remove tinfoil from rotten bouquets.

Out of sight, a bell calls children from classrooms.
Their play sounds the same in every country, every time.
I leave a pebble, stolen from Top Withens, at her head.
The dead can't speak unless we listen.

A crystal vase holds rain and dead heather,
a bee is skating on the algae, a drunk dancer,
dipping down, she can't keep her face above water.
I scoop her out with one finger. She doesn't sting.

EXISTENTIAL CRISIS AS APOCALYPSE

The pictures aren't there. In the sky. Plough Seven Sisters Orion. If a burning rock hit Earth and humanity dissolved, quick as a blink, there would be no memory of the pictures in the sky. There would be no one to remember. In school, the teacher—who I will later realise was some sort of sadist—lists ways humanity could come to an end. *Pandemic, comets, super volcano, nuclear war, the next ice age, a robot uprising.* We write postcards to the Queen of England asking her to shut Sellafield. The Irish government posts iodine tablets to every household to counteract leaked radiation. That same teacher tells us they contain cyanide, so that when the nuclear apocalypse starts our parents can kill us like the Goebbels. I eye that packet of tablets for the next nine years. A trend of disaster dystopia NOW films appear during the 1990s. Perhaps growing up under the threat of the cold war heightened the fatalism of the collective consciousness. CGI has outstripped the limits of traditional film making. Now, the imagination is the limit. Between jingle-laden ad breaks for Guinness and state sponsored turf flogging, *Deep Impact* and *Armageddon* show me the end is nigh. Even the children's illustrated bible doesn't have a happy ending. Dead Johnny Cash sings from the stereo: A white horse, a pale horse. Stars out my window feel like the holding of breath before tears. Hellfire. Church choir. Change: body / brain. A black pup barks at the moon.

SEX ED. 2004

Spin it

Pull it

Flick it

Twist it

Bop it

YOW

D.O.S.E[1]

Staying up until pink tinges the horizon, your eyes sting
and you're so giddy laughs come on each breath.

Snorting packets of sherbet with your friends.

Finding out Columbus discovered America.
Finding out Columbus didn't discover America.

Jumping from the pier into the Atlantic,
arrow straight rise of chill over your head, basal shiver,
feeling heat in only your mouth and your vulva.

Lying on a roundabout looking at the clouds,
not knowing if they're moving or you are.

Cycling downhill on a bike with no brakes.

Kissing
with your whole body.

Making love to yourself all night long.

---

1   *The four primary chemicals in the brain that effect happiness are Dopamine, Oxytocin, Serotonin, and Endorphins.*
Dose is Irish slang for an annoying person.

LEAVING HOME (AGAIN)

I post my keys through the letterbox, and empty
my account on two books of poems and a can

of Diet Coke. I read on the Rosie and chain smoke.
The Liffey is green, salt-soaked, heaving from trickle

to spring, now she's leaving. The smell—tar, kelp, Chinese food—
summertime. Vis-vests are hacking

at the new Luas line. Facebook pings FOMO
future date. The gutter glitters with piss.

I flaneur, tongue tucked in cheek, spy on small routines.
Reminisce: Sea-mist noon mornings. Nescafé

and limescale in a mug. Library warmth,
raindrops on slanted glass like children

on a slide. G&Ts with someone else's lipstick on
the rim. The sky above the boardwalk turning black

to orange to pink, the ding of the first bus home.
Singing, and swinging off the bars of the Ha'penny

letting go
of what took so long to find.

My pockets are light with lack
of keys, change. There is no plan tonight.

EXISTENTIAL CRISIS AS ADDICTION
> *Every form of addiction is bad, no matter whether the narcotic be alcohol, morphine or idealism.*
> — C.G. Jung

In the space of nights, I lose years. Wake
to find them in the crumpled pillows of lost boys.
Mad woman in attic bedrooms. City twinkling
through the Velux. Urban fox nipping at my heels.

Dogged lust. Get into difficulty
in cocktails thick as canal water.
Rooftop yards like cattle crushes,
only stinking of Amber Leaf.

Smoke the monster out. Tip the glass
to death's dilating pupil. The birthing cervix
of the Earth. A fat caterpillar, on a chaise longue,
blowing smoke rings to the mirror.

Four hours before classes not attended. Look out
to that set-your-watch fox cutting across the roof,
bumper-car traffic, buses wedged, pavements
wobbly with suits swimming downstream.

Write poetry. Shift poets. Fall in love with both. Take
a shot. Take a picture. Turn the other cheek
(for a better angle). Post a selfie. Postpostpostmodern.
Post-language/truth/love. Nothing exists.

My reflection is out of focus. Veil thin. Barely there.

GIRL

I shrugged off *girl*
wore myself out
like an ill-fitting dress.

The body, does it flick like a switch:
a baby, blood, love?
A girl inside-out: womanhood.
Like my reversible childhood doll.
One way she was little red riding hood
folded in on herself she was Grandma
though even that was an illusion
the wolf wearing the old woman's
skin as a mask, belly full,
ready to fuck little red.

Is it fuckability
that makes the girl?
When I dated an older man, he won
every argument with experience.

No evolution,
like a Pokémon levelling up
Girl →→→ Woman.

Now I reserve the right
not to know
what is best for me.

BIRTHDAY

It's March
again
I am aging.

The day, grey
and bloated as a dead seal.

Candle-less wish.
Seaside stable.
Silver steed.
Twist of leather,
slap of flank.
Soft underhand,
sturdy as stone walls.
Smell of sawdust,
sweet grass.

A trot, spit
of salt drops.

I've been feeling like flinging myself
in the sea, like peeling my skin off,
like getting a fist quick across my lips,
hungry for shock to shake up
the beat of the day(to)day humdrum.

The vacuum of equine eyes.
Steam plumes from velvet black holes.

Strain on stirrup, push to gallop.
We ride the whip of the wind.

I grip—
or forget to—
we slip,
spill

*

Sand and blood swirl down
the shower drain.
Across my hip a nebula sprawls,
all purple, crimson, gold—
damage knitting itself away
cells healing as stars form.

ECLIPSING BLOOD MOON

The blood moon rises, half eclipsed.
My joints click as my weight shifts
from hip to hip and back.
Underfoot, pebbles roll and clack.

There's a tidal pull in me tonight.
The inside of my thigh wet,
wrong as an oil slick,
sick with what didn't happen.

The waves lick the shore almost silently.
Rapid wane.
The moon runs
her month in minutes.

My guiltless cigarette wipes out the dark,
orange disc alone in celestial black.

CHASING FRUIT FLIES AROUND THE HOUSE

with tea towel and a can of Raid.
I light a cigarette and think,
I'll make a blowtorch, burn them all!

I may as well move house for all
the hope I have of getting rid
of them today or—I can't go
calling an exterminator
on a few fruit flies, that would be
overreacting *surely,* like
calling an ambulance for a
comparatively mild bout of
suicidal ideation.

They hop from wall to wall and back
again and again. I'd love a
tennis racket with no holes in,
show them the joy of being flung
aimlessly from side to side.

BANG BANG synaptic explosions,
tiny bullet ideas, all
consuming, flitting about my
brain. Intangible, they came from
where, to dart about the inside
of my head as if it were an
empty room filling up with flies
banging against the plasterboard

of my skull like my meninges
were one strip of sticky paper.

They're still getting in, I seal the
windows, gaffer tape the doors. I
stuff myself, bleach-soaked cotton
in my ears, thread through my tear
stung lips, tar my eyes crease to duct.
One whip crack—*wapush*—of cloth at
a time, I carpet the floor with
their cracked bodies, legs stuck up
spindly black as neglected pubes.
Still the buzzing fills the room.

STARTING FIRES

Tending the fire alone
on a March day, daffodils sinking
under hailstones' icy weight.
The wood hisses like a wild cat.
The coal will not catch.

I have doused myself in oil
to soften my shell.
Smell of lemon and almonds.
Sweet to counteract the bitter tickle

of the ash that smudges my hands
as I use the tongs to draw out the red
centre of the coal, like cracking
an egg, desperate for the yolk.

Soft as soil, the embers give way to metal,
Forceps, babies squeezed through birth.
Branding cow hides, burning hair and beef sizzle.
Knuckles screwed, limbs pulled apart.

The flames begin to nurture a good heat.
Our home is soft and warm for another night.

THE DOCTOR (WHO?) WAS A WOMAN

I'm a Timelord, now: two hearts.
An everyday biological anomaly.
Feel the double tic-tic when the wand
is pressed to me. A clock with the future
intact. I'm a sci-fi reality. Genes releasing
each scene to come. The past is etched
into each beat of my belly. Across my breasts
grow saplings, branches; that vein is your family tree.

We, now, not a me. We're imaginary.
Tight jeans, taste for salt, bus stop throw-up.
A secret, a hush, and a photo of a bean.
I feel like I made you up.

CHARLOTTE PERKINS-GILMAN

From beneath the wallpaper she
can see there is *no reason to suffer*
and yet, being one with a *slight
hysterical tendency,* she creeps,
keeping hidden from husband,
from the nursery, from herself.

> *Live as domestic a life*
> *As possible*
> *Have your child with you*
> *All the time.*

Crying *at nothing,* unhinging
shoulders, hips crawling like
a bug, flat and frantic under
the yellow wash of daily life
an effort it is to do what little
that she does, that she can't do,
not to stick to the wall, inhaling
paste, dust, her doctor's orders
until her mind is as stuck
as plaster to paste to paper.

> *Have but two hours' intellectual*
> *Life a day.*
> *And never touch*
> *Pen, brush or pencil*
> *As long as you live.*

She could free herself yet,
tear away from the walls
jump through barred windows,
but *a step like that is improper
and might be misconstrued.*

NEBULA (OR, PREMONITION)

Will you come in the night?
A comet, pure fire.

Sweat of Hadean summer,
sheen like petrol on a puddle.

I shed my clothes,
like a snake's old skin

slip into the water
douse myself
like I'm trying to quench a flame.

Light-laced water mottles
the wave of my belly.
Veins on a leaf held to the sun.
The tide is coming in.

Effacing ozone layer.
I split apart. The atmosphere
burns up. A star falling.

The Earth rises to meet you.

II. Big House

We all live in a house on fire, no fire department to call; no way out, just the upstairs window to look out of while the fire burns the house down with us trapped, locked in it.
— *Tennessee Williams*

It is easier for a man to burn down his own house than to get rid of his prejudices.
— *Roger Bacon*

CHARACTER DEVELOPMENT
I went to the place and found the whole house a seething mass of flames. I at once saw that all was hopeless. A fire brigade would be powerless, so firmly had the flames gripped the entire building. I could do nothing but stand by and await the end with the same feelings one has when standing by the open grave of a very dear friend.

— Account of steward James Reilly via George Moore, The Morning Post, 1923

Pre-breakdown
The Clarion Hotel, fka Sligo District Asylum, 2011

The gut-rolling hill of the town
pushes the stone hotel skywards.
Cloak skimming my heels, I drink
Bacardi and coke from a champagne
flute. Debutante lady of luxury,
I'm eighteen and anticipating.
Two decades since the last patients were
shaken out like a bundle of stale washing.
Look at the lawns laid out like cloths of heaven
about to be whipped from under my feet.

MID-BREAKDOWN
Moore Hall, Mayo, 2012

Through Coillte forestry the house peeps,
sockets hollow, stone facade threatening
to crumble, abandoned as a burned-out car.

In the woods, I'm nineteen and thinking
of Kate Winslet kissing Snape, an ache
in my calf and I moan *If we were in England
there'd be a tearoom by now. Fluffy scones,
somewhere to piss.* My mother rolls her eyes,
says *Big House means something else, to us,
than period dramas and the National Trust.*

We stop at the Moore family plot,
beloved landlords, it's still said
not one in their estate
lost bed nor life to famine.

Tucked behind is the cillín, ivy knots
over unholy ground, unknown babies' place
of rest marked by soil and stone, (lucky ones)
not a slab over hollow/ tank/ hiding place.
While the boys had their knuckles, arses bust
open on a Brother's belt, girls—like me—fell
down rabbit holes steep as laundry chutes, wrists tied
in dirty sheets, landing in a bed of their own making.

Nothing new in the silhouette of a Big House
on the hill. Centuries of unblinking windows,

ascending staircases to a divided heaven.
Swapping one yoke for another is easy
when you're born to live on your knees.

Post-breakdown
Nazareth House, Sligo, 2019

Looping with the baby in the buggy, I am thinking
of our barbarous history. Children without pram-pushing
mammies, deposited like pebbles, scattered to Houses
like this, to be dragged up, moved on, some whole lives
behind state walls. I am not thinking of the fair
in the square named for peace, where pre-baby,
I lay swollen in the daisies, air buzzing with bongos,
guitars, a chorus of children. Rice, meat, and spices
spooned into paper bowls. This fought-for feeling
of (provisional) joy, floating like pollen in
the sunbeams sneaking through the branches
that border yet another House on the hill.

What use is my memory
of a day when no one was speaking
like they do on the internet. *As a mother*
I know what it is to be other.
Ha!
The newborn directs my gaze.
My prayers contrived, and, not to mention,
a bit fucking late.

A HISTORY OF MENTAL HEALTH CARE IN FIVE ACTS
To compromise between the sad, euphonious word, asylum, and the modern, physical-jerk words, mental hospital, I shall call this particular place – the Big House.
— Hanna Greally, bird's nest soup, 1971

Act for the Erecting of Houses of Correction and for the Punishment of Rogues, Vagabonds, Sturdy Beggars, and Other Lewd and Idle Persons (1634)

Rid the streets of rogues: starved curs snarling
in tune with the undercurrent of rebellion.

A pandemic of poverty, land luteal
with opportunity for work/houses.

Hands, raw from unwillingness,
cracked open in a question. How?

Gift: Usefulness.
Useful: Sturdy beggars.

Gift: distraction of falling.
Rescued: Women.

Gift: salvation.
Saved: aged, infirm, mad, unwanted.

Gift: laudanum, infinite rest.
Sucklers: infants of the catholic poor.

In the belly of this industry: cells of Lunatics
loaded with chains, frantic as drowning cats.

IRISH LUNATIC ASYLUMS FOR THE POOR ACT (1817)

There is nothing so shocking as madness
in the cabin of the peasant

where the man is out labouring
in the fields for his bread, and the care
of the woman of the house is scarcely
sufficient for the attendance on the children
when a strong young man or woman gets the complaint,
the only way they have to manage is by making a hole
in the floor of the cabin not high enough for the person
to stand up in, with a crib over it to prevent
his getting up, the hole is about five feet deep,
they give this wretched being his food
there, and there he generally dies

Of all human calamity
I know of none equal to this

*

Before we had no Lunatic Asylum
there was to be a certain number
of Lunatic cells annexed to every county gaol

*

The manner in which the Lunatics are treated
in the House of Industry in Dublin:

>noise is the most terrible and destructive thing
>in cases of madness
>yet some of these wretched
>people were screeching
>sleep to others was
>utterly impossible
>that they could have rest

>dirt, noise, confusion

a place more calculated to occasion madness
than to cure it

*

a view to the recovery
of the patient

Desperate cases
little or no chance of recovery:
>remove from them causes of irritation
>regulate the degrees of restraint

provide occupation for the convalescent

*

considerable proportion of the entire number are idiots,
mostly become so, having been a lunatic
then sinking into idiocy

*

accommodation afforded to the insane will appear
to be such as we should not appropriate for our dog
    exposed
    extremities of the weather
    the death of two patients
     thirteen cells to be occupied by thirty-three
    a state of furious insanity

*

The usual mode of restraint:
    hands under their knees,
    fastening them with manacles
    bolts about their ankles
    a chain over all, and then
    fastening them to a bed

In this state
they have continued for years
utterly incapable of rising

*

The general want

A woman with the corpse of her child,
left upon her knees for two days;
it was almost in a state of putridity

Keeper of the Lunatics claimed an exclusive dominion
over the females confided to his charge,
which he exercised in the most abominable manner

*

provision for poor Lunatics
was always opposed
on account of the expenses

the misery of madness
not air enough
not space enough for air

*

I did often beg of a physician
to try medicine,
which he very seldom would do

We now receive no cases
but urgent cases of private distress,
or such as inconvenience the public

*

pressure   increasing

lower classes
afflicted with mental derangement

there should be   District Asylums
containing   Lunatics

the public ought to contribute
to the cure of malady
alleviation of wretchedness
so deeply interesting to humanity

DANGEROUS LUNATICS ACT (1838)
For the Better Prevention of Crime Being Committed by the Insane

Patients shall be treated
with gentleness.
Restraint (when necessary)
shall be moderate.

> Strap limbs with soft leather.
> Break only the most slender arms.

Avoid any harsh
or intemperate language.
Attendants must
(by steadiness, kindness and gentleness)
contribute to that system of moral
government, upon which the value
of the Asylum depends.

> Rape the incompetent.
> Leave the disruptive to hang.

Observe most unvarying kindness
towards the lunatics.

Mental Treatment Act (1945)

Our land bears the memory of hunger
on its back like a skeletal monkey.
Still, the fields show their ribs.
Cupboards dusty with Emergency.
Éire's arms, newborn, too scrawny
to carry the weight of the unwanted.

We haven't the luxury of jobs
lost, more mouths falling open
at our table. There'll be no community
caring for anyone without the ~~asylum~~ hospital.

What will we do with the ~~lunatics~~ mentally ill?
Where will we put ~~the vagrants, idiots,~~
our unclaimed?

Case Study: Anecdotal Evidence From An Ordinary Provincial Mental Hospital (1940s/50s)

HANNA

I should not have stayed more than a year in the Big House. 'A nervous breakdown' by proxy. No voluntary status for inmates.

MOTHER

Remember it is not your fault, be good, don't give any cause for complaint.

HANNA

Mother, I want you to claim me out.

OTHER

You'll never get out.

MOTHER

That's it, dear. The woman always pays.

HANNA

There is something very sinister going on.

OTHER

Nobody wants you.

HANNA

Salts in the morning, sedatives for the restless in the day, and the inevitable liquid paraffin in the evening.

OTHER

You write lovely letters.

> HANNA

ECT. A captive in a free society.

> MOTHER

Remember it is not your fault, be good, don't give any cause for complaint.

> OTHER

You'll never get out.

> HANNA

Thousands of letters to relatives near and far no results, cannot leave, legally, without their help.

> OTHER

Nobody wants you.

> HANNA

[Other] had of course written her own version of what happened—

> MOTHER

That's it, dear. The woman always pays.

> OTHER

Destructive mania.

> HANNA

—the disproportionate, fantastic, exaggerated headlines of my misdeeds.

Mental Health Act (2001)
(or, Revolving Door)

This is the door you come in.
Just five min, a quick chat.
Plead with the white coat's pen.
Take these pills for the rest of your life.

This was the door they came in.
Prostrate, plugged into the mains.
A needle of pig in the flank
brings a good long sleep.
Heads hangdog for a slice.
A miracle! A new kind of pain.

CARE/COMMUNITY

> *My generation can't afford houses, my generation can't afford to have children, my generation are either leaving the country or jumping in rivers, that's my generation, man.*
> — Blindboy Boatclub, The Late Late Show, 2016

A Luxury Escape

The lift fits one family at a time,
or two professional men
their luggage separately ascending
carried in the fists of a man on his eleventh hour
(today) of his zero hour contract.

The kids run ahead through the foyer,
Thursday, they finally stopped asking to go home.
Mini croissants folded into schoolbags
to be nibbled on the bus. Over filter coffee
and bitty juice, a guest's eyeball rolls from their damp
hair to uniform shoes. Meaning nothing, she supposes.
They just weren't expecting—over breakfast buffet—
such a sight, assume such domesticity should be
reserved for the home. Wouldn't that be nice?

Lifeboat

City gone to the dogs, all Airbnbs and refugees.
Haven't we enough trouble with our own junkies,
single mothers and their brats getting it all for free,
without opening up to any beggar at the border.

You heard about the lad from back the way,
was in my son's class in school, same age I was
when my young fella was born. Word was he lost
the work, back home with rent too steep,
he'd a hurling injury from when he was a pup,
they say the waitlist got too much. Anyway,
hung himself from the crossbeams of his mammy's
attic. God save us, if we can't even mind our own
and more are coming. Will be worse now with,
what's it, global warming and brexit. We know
there weren't enough lifeboats on the titanic.

Only a Mother Could

Damp dawns buckle her fingers, filling the kettle
out of the question. Even when he's able, or has a notion,
he makes weak tea. Watching Corrie with the dinner
on their laps is not the worst, though not how his father
imagined their later years. A pack of grandkids to spoil
was what he wished, broken-hearted not to live
to see them. He'd have been immortal waiting.
Some consolation he didn't know she'd had her fill
of children with their own. All she was after now
was the boy's happiness. She's not the first woman
to be left wanting. No space for prayers these days.
Even if she's more likely to get an answer doing that
than by calling the hospital again. The boy, man
now, liked the place well enough, but *you have to think
of the funds. Patients happier at home. There's nothing
to be done.* The years, the sky, turning golden.

You Say ~~Promise~~ Potato I Say ~~Threat~~ Tomato

I try to keep my footsteps down,
their clatter is a bullet of a nag
to his temple. *Nag nag*

nag nag I'm an old horse now
and the glue bottle's not looking so bad.
His mind is pole-vaulting

indecision. Says it might be tonight.
We're living in the continued splintering of time.
Both forks in the road are closed for maintenance.

One way we go on—another baby, move house,
perhaps go on holidays. But today I find him
hanging bug-eyed and frothing. Tomorrow

he's bathing in red. Next week, he's under a park bench,
a gruesome discovery for a passerby walking their dog.
I've rung all the numbers.

Shakespeare's monkeys of helplines.
It's no use. I'm the girl who cried ____
but all those other days were cubs

and today definitely has fangs.
If it were serious, they'd already be dead.
Go to A&E when there's been an attempt.

Drop a woman in a lake.
If she drowns, we were wrong.
If the lake is someone she loves, too bad.

I think of black dresses, miniature suits.
Condolences from the fat hands of strangers.
I think of not going at all.

Wife pirouettes into widow.
His variety act, a promise
he can't seem to keep. Actors

trying out scenes. We play
in stasis. Always the same:
he can't hear my scream.

III. The Ethics of Cats

Nature is a haunted house
—Emily Dickinson

When Rome burned, the emperor's cats still expected to be fed on time.
—Seanan McGuire

(RE)WILD

This infinity of weeks is flying.
Elastic time snaps back to childhood summers.

Somewhere, deep in memory's foundation,
I see a buzzing hive, a sky dizzy with birds.

Now, you paw pears, raspberries,
slices of sweet tomato.

You laugh at the cat's lawn acrobatics,
watch your first swallow loop the open field.

I scroll news sites on my phone,
hold fear in my mouth like an almost rotten fruit.

We plant hazel, willow, oak.
The too few bees zig-zag between the blossoms.

Summers will unfold
sooner than we expect.

THE WALKOUT

She saw it coming: the cold pit
in the bed, his irregular hours,
strolling in with expectation
for dinner, a rub of her legs.

She wondered if he had a second family,
like in the films: a better-dressed wife
pops up at a patriarch's funeral,
towing two children with his eyes.

She heard the door in the morning
—like a departure for work,
imagined dew on the windscreen,
pink sky, squabbling birds—
after a night of straying, his soft steps
on the stairs a too-needed snuggle,
sour breath close to hers.

When it happened, she didn't know
it would be the last time, that tired cliché.
Her hands in his hair, the rumble of his throat.

When she woke, an indent in the pillow
was all that remained. She felt nothing
but normal as she packed lunches,
swept floors, filled bowls.

In the weeks that followed, she told herself he'd return.
She wasn't the first woman scorned, to be a doormat
to an ungrateful—No, she stopped herself.
He'd be back. Eventually, the child asked,
mum, where's the cat?

I DIDN'T NAME YOU FOR A KING

nor ancestor. Not for an author,
nor aspirational abstract.

On the documentary—kept on a loop
more than The Den or any rags to riches
Disney Princess spinning into fate—
there was an elephant. A bull calf
to a matriarch. Slow to walk, his legs curled
from the snug of his mother. He was nudged
and led, his family holding off on their search
for food, water. Not his mother alone,
but all of them. Until the unlikely boy
stretched his boundless legs and strode.

Look, what they showed us
of love beyond ourselves.

Scientists, yes, but also a child who never doubted
animals could love, whose faith lay in what had not
been discovered yet but what could be, if importance
was bestowed upon it. I'd wanted to do what I saw
on the telly: save the tigers, elephants, whales.
Even without a voice like David Attenborough's.
I knew nothing of Oxbridge, or my own limitations.
Later, I thought conservation a luxury
for those not preoccupied with their own survival.
(I was wrong.)

Twelve years before your birth.
In the Mill Street carpark
of our town, grimy then, as I was
with love and eyeliner. A circus
held two elephants behind blue rope.
The sort I knew from pulling calves
(the cow kind) from their mothers.
Easy for a teenage girl (with both too much
and not enough confidence) to nip under.
Indignant at their confinement, but more
than that, delighted in their proximity.

Daring myself closer: I was in Amboseli,
and not Castlebar. One wrapped his trunk
around my middle. I cooed to him
as I would a horse. How easily
the animal could lift me, and not let go,
but didn't. He ran the bristled nostrils
along the netting of my gothic costume,
deemed me holder of neither food nor threat,
then let me go, to slip back to relative safety,
elated and jittery at my own stupidity.

My own conviction than an intelligent animal
wouldn't hurt me. When I knew well already
the capabilities of supposedly smarter animals.
Never mind one whose interaction with humans
had left him in a carpark, in Castle-fucking-bar,
sludgy potholes underfoot, the air a fug
of Subway spices pouring from a nearby extractor fan.

Where even in June, as it was then, the weather
can't have been milder than 14 °C. Hardly the image
from the telly, a dry savanna, wavy with heat and static.

I forgot about the elephants. The tigers, whales,
endangered birds. Distracted as I was by love,
grimy eyeliner, poetry: the filthy joy of independence.

But when you began your mammalian
curl and kick. Making an animal
of me again. I remembered all that love
I'd known once for each creature and with it,
the grief of disappearing species.

Anyway, back to your namesake.
He would go on to surprise again,
wounded once, his family knit
around him, undeterred by gunshots
and later again he wandered
undetected for a decade
before reemerging,
not lost to poachers at all,
but strong, beautiful, a joy
to those who thought him lost.

Those years belong to him,
making his unobserved way in the world.
Solid with the care of his beginning.

PULLING BACK THE DRAPES ON A DECEMBER MORNING

The baby curls his hands up like question marks. Asks,
dark? Blinking sleep, he peers out the window, shouts
moon! at the lightbulb's belly reflected in the glass.

I smile, shake my head, flick the switch.
Twirls of turf smoke cut through the mist.
Across the way, the school windows are lit.

Coffee steam clears my sinuses. We watch the sun
sneak up over a hill of spruce. Any day now, the turn
will come, we'll welcome light with the crack of curtain.

IN THE BELLY

A cross appears like a blessing.
My body sighs.

*

The snowdrop hangs
her head like she's mistaken
the frost-lit soil for sun.
Something in her instinct
draws her down.

When spring sets in
the only evidence
of her short life
is a lawn alight
with her absence.

*

My small son rushes from clump to clump.
I pluck thread from the bog for the crosses
of Imbolc, of Brigid. He cries as his hands
overflow with earth, pebbles, peat.
Centuries won't fit in his small paws.
I weave memorials to the winter
now that it has passed (thank god).
We are faithless. Heritage is as hazy
as a blue line promising a cross.

*

I hear crying. Beside me,
my toddler slumbers softly.
Yet the crying comes, like layers
of trees becoming mulch.
As the tearless nights multiple,
I flood and empty
like a worked-out bog hole.

NEUTRALITY
Blacksod Lighthouse, Co. Mayo

Here, first it hits

granite squares its shoulders
to the forces
wind, wave

black clouds advance
like a terrible fleet

this theatre of stone and salt
under watch of one
long blinking eye

                              1944: rapidly falling barometer
                                                repeating call
                                    across fractured frontiers
                                            check and repeat

                                    a warning that signalled
                                        the start of the end

here, the coast bursts open
its knuckles on the sea's jagged grin
teeth shatter in the spray

rock ground to sand
bags filled and piled
a barricade bracing itself for breach

amphibious
attempt to adapt

pressure
repeating call
falling barometer

check and repeat

now
another century turns
an over-the-shoulder glance

threat lurks like a riptide

here, the first spied hint of
answer to
prayer for
—light

The ocean unhinges its jaw
to swallow us whole

Here, it hits again

IN THE NAME OF

Love, you're a bastard.
Is it any wonder we fell out?

All the same, you needn't have been so harsh.
Dick dipping in like a painter's brush.
Youth too brief for monochrome.

The bed heavy with drink,
and you, heavier. I begged for it.

Making a riddle of want
and safety. Incompatible bedfellows.

After you
I grew coy as a predator.
Only one of us could survive.

Now you return, tail tucked
so firmly between your legs
it must have displaced
the head up your arse.

You dare to ask me to forgive
the terrible things
I did
in your name.

THE KITTEN IS IN HEAT

She's yowling with a face full of *Felix*.
I thought the jellied fish might shush her.

My cat is horny and keeps stuffing her face.
Every friend I tell says *same girl, same.*

She wraps around my neck, a sad snake.
All she wants is love. *Same girl, same.*
Google tells me to try penetrating her
with a Q-tip, but you have to draw the line somewhere.

I bring her to have her bits out. She has no say in it.
She was a stray, malnourished, a weak chest.
Pregnancy would be a disaster, the vet says.
(*Same girl, same.*)

I tickle her ears, shush her
crooning instinctual calls.
Hush hush now,
soon you won't want at all.

CRESCENDO

The first time I saw him, all those years ago upstairs in a musty old Dublin pub, he rose from the crowd and strode into focus. All the things I had been told to wait for. All the Disney princes, the boys next door, the guys mothers warn about, Phoebus verbally sparring with Esmerelda in Notre Dame, Heathcliff's shriek into the Yorkshire night, Jack Sparrow and Aragorn on peeling plastic posters, Nick Cave's vampiric intensity, my childhood sweetheart picking apples, James Dean's white t-shirt and leather jacket, every carved set of initials in the school desk, Janet singing *touch me* under Rocky's golden underwear & Brad's tighty-whities, Prince Eric's unbuttoned shirt, David Attenborough's voice, Ted pulling Sylvia's red ribbon from her hair, the impossible romantic fantasies, Hugh Grant and Colin Firth crashing through the window of a Greek restaurant, Jess Mariano lending Rory books with notes in the margins, Leo Decaprio and the sweat condensing on the car window, Simba and Nala rolling in the grass, Orpheus following Eurydice to the underworld. Every promise the romantic and erotic world had failed to deliver rushed in and collided as he paced the room and let his eyes stall on mine and that, I'm afraid, was that.

PLAYING HOUSE

We play at it:
Marriage.

You fix my son's hat
when it slips over his eyes
as he introduces you to the moon
when it peeps from behind bruised clouds,
like an old friend who's been missing.

While I soak the smell of your
sleep(less) hot sheets from my skin,
you read about pirates & diggers,
fix shakily broken cranes,
the boy stuff I fail to understand.

I get quotes from the classics stuck
in my head as if they were lines from power
ballads blasted in the car:

Beginning and end this abyss the sun and other
(shut up!) dramatic shit like that
which possessed me
when I was young and committed
to the act of loving.

Now, we don't stay out late
like we did years ago.
We rush back to relieve the babysitter.

You pull the bins down to the main road,
load the dishwasher while I rock sleep to my toddler.

A child in the buggy, your arm slung casually
over my shoulders. What could be more normal,
to a passer-by, than a young couple out
for a late-night walk, pushing a fretful kid?

It's nice, the roleplaying.
You perform your duties well.
Make jokes about your hoodie being husband material.
Close the cupboard doors when I leave them open.
I laugh unselfconsciously, remind you to drink enough
water to ward off the hangover.
We know, now, the trick to love
is not looking it in the eye.

My hand on your jaw, your back,
yours on my thighs.
I watch your pupils dilate as I come.

It's so nice, playing make-believe.
Later, over clink of kettle and pots, you say
This is nice, is this what it's supposed to be like?
And I freeze
in case the house falls down around me.

TWO MAMS TALKING
For Sinead

I have a fantasy about falling down the stairs—
                                —imagine that, a broken leg

A couple of days in bed—
                                      —a whole summer!

Or a few days on the psychiatric ward.
                           I know someone who did and
                              (would you believe)
                           gave out they were bored.
                             Nothing to do but lie
                           in bed and read books all day.

The dream.
                                          The dream!

THE CAT KILLS A MOUSE

Which elegant predator is the perpetrator?
Soft friends with whom we share our home.
We'd named it, scurrying from behind the skirting board.
Disease carrier, sure, but look at those petal-like ears.
Is the mouse going to be ok? My son asks and I know,
as much as I might want to, I can't tell him *yes*.

I say the mouse's body doesn't work anymore,
no, the cats aren't naughty, it's their nature.
We will bury the mouse and give its energy back
to the soil, so plants can grow, and flower to feed the bees.

There's nothing to be afraid of I lie, as if my own
childhood nights weren't marked by fear of pets
rundown, parental heart attacks, nuclear malfunctions.

All three years of him is tight with worry now.
How will the mouse's mammy find him in the ground?
I've fucked up this basic task. If only I hadn't let him
name the pest, encouraged his boundless love
for creatures. I as good as set him up for loss.

At night, when the scuttling mice in the attic
spook him from sleep, I rock him like his younger self,
when my body was the answer to his restless tears.
I whisper *it's ok,* as if fear can be loved away.

EVOLUTION

Cats are no more natural than plastic.
Felis catus, the littlest ones,
the sort who flush toilets online.

We [extracted] a naturally occurring
feline / fossil fuel
and [processed]
produced
an ideal.

look at my beautiful
cat. Her name in rhinestones on her collar.
It looks just like the real thing!
We are terribly efficient.

*

I was sure this was an exact
and brilliant metaphor. Yet
again, I am spectacularly
incorrect. Scientifically,
cats are useless.

Cats are remarkably similar
to their wild cousins.
Their breeding is not selected
or controlled like dogs, cattle, horses,
other once wild pack animals.

They don't provide
us with milk, wool, transport.

It is unlikely the wild ancestors of cats
were captured and harnessed for their mousing
abilities. Dogs would have been more efficient.
It is more likely that wild cats hung
around human settlements and fed on the vermin
we generated. Friendly and clever, our ancestors
tolerated theirs. If domestication took place,
the instigator is uncertain.

*

Cats are perfectly capable
of living wild, or feral, to use
the term for a creature once captive,
living as if wild. A cat may identify
as a wild animal. Or it may identify
as your baby, leaping to your arms
at the sound of a ring pull can.

*

A cat chooses the owner,
although it is worth mentioning
cats are not known for drowning children
in bog holes or dropping off their humans
at a shelter when their landlord says NO PETS.
However, a cat may abscond to the neighbour's

without leaving so much as a note.
It may live comfortably two fields over
in the house where the mam buys wet
cat food, not the dry shite from Lidl,
while you plaster Facebook and the community
centre window with MISSING posters.

*

Cats live alongside humans. Our care
does not constitute our control of them.
An environmental disaster (of course),
but they're not domesticated, not properly.
They keep us a little bit wild.

YES, AND BACK AGAIN

I'm sitting in a Queen Anne chair by the bay window,
looking over a lawn of grass, dandelions, clover,

fat thrushes pulling worms up like fighting spaghetti.
Word has come in over twitter that he's dead in the war.

Somewhere hot and crumbling, like all battlefields
known to our generation. Nobody dies in the rain.

I'm listening to more birdsong than I've heard in years.
It radiates from the beech, sycamore, willow

of this one-time Big House with its walkway
to swans floating on the still green lake.

It's feeling a little too *How many miles to Babylon.*
Big Houses and war and things from the past.

My milk is drying up, my usefulness done.
Someone served me breakfast.

Once, the dead man called me a goddess. I laughed,
said *shut the fuck up, I'm an atheist.* He blushed.

I can't write poems in this luxury. I've no right to it.
Residencies feel like a kind of cultured charity.

I may as well paint Jesus, make a martyr
of him for coins and a pat on the head.

Aching with principles. I'd grown out of that.
He joked he'd a death wish. I kissed him to hush.

I barely knew him. My tits are hot balls of pain.
On the gravel drive, a thrush drops its worm.

CODE-SWITCHING
*I still don't know the difference
between a bloke and a chap*
— Billy Collins

The difference between

a bloke and a chap

is inheritance.

FAT CATS

are lining their stomachs with dairy and beef,
diesel and pesticides, national roads and natural gas

with windfarms and school meal plans, Samaritan boxes
on newsagent tills, legal aid fees and state pension

shavings, bubble-popping electric bills, with rentals
and rentals and more rentals, with satisfaction.

The fat cats can't fit through the flap. All the birds
in the garden are dead. The rivers don't run,

the flypaper doesn't even catch pollen.
The hedgerows are quiet, unwavering:

there's nothing to hear until somebody asks
How did you let that cat get so fat?

HOT CAT DAD

He's Thomas O'Malley, right up my alley,
this cat, man, how I go for the scruffy,
unexpectedly lovely, mewling and stalking
the grounds. When there's danger, he mauls
me, says he's marking his territory.
The sofa and my pillow has his stink.
I can't get his hairs out of the sink.

I'm told cats don't love you back: *Stop projecting!*
He only hangs around cause you feed him!
They think he's Shirkhan but wipe rusty fluff
away, he's Bagheera. Protector, exasperated, quicker
to laugh than he cares to admit. He's the Tiger
Who Came to Tea. Uninvited, welcomed
in like an old friend. He's Mufasa, Simba chewing
his ear off before dawn. Mane ruffled and luxurious,
sun rich. I want his teeth on the scruff of my neck.

ZIGGY

Flotsam like, she washes up at our house
after a storm. Bedraggled and sneezing,

one eye weeping and gummed shut,
the other a sea-green bean. Three bowls already

to fill, there's no room at the inn! But God loves
an outcast or at the very least, I do. Lungs crackling

like a new fire, she knocks herself over with a sneeze.
Malnourished, blind in one eye, she's likely on borrowed

time. The vet bill costs more than my car. With the
asymmetrical gaze of Stardust, her marmalade zigzag,

she spends a year biting my ankles for *Felix*, noosing
herself around Cat Dad. She's a school-run stowaway

turn interactive *show & tell* surprise. 'til one autumn
morning, I mistake her for a heap of wet leaves.

Curled on the roadside, nose to tarmac
like it's another cat's bum. She looks up to me

unseeing, sea-bean replaced by a balloon
of crimson. Still, her shaky chest heaves.

The vet does X-rays, a drip, a sedative, a snip.
Miracle. No damage done; except the one good eye.

Another groan-summoning bill, then she's home,
bumping noses with doorframes, eating the finest

of tinned mush in gravy, sharpening claws on my chin.
She's either the luckiest or most unlucky cat in the world.

It's all about perspective, really,
which is ironic, considering she has none.

IN THE BELLY (CONT.)

All night I piss on sticks that deliver
another chance.
I wake to fresh grief,
a full bladder.

EXISTENTIAL CRISIS AS ANTHROPOCENE

The forest bathing experience at the budget spa is fitting.
No more a forest than the chlorine-sticky hot tub
is a spring. Lines of bristling towers staccato
my vision. Thoughts uninterrupted by traffic or birdsong.

I walk barefoot from the sauna
to a clearing. Quarry gravel indents
my soles. I am thirty tomorrow.
A mother, an ex-wife, a lover.

Chilly with this Irish March, I retreat
to the body-warm pool, our public solitude.
His wet kiss closes my lids.
Overhead a crow shrieks.

At home, the cat kills another mouse, fat
on the detritus of what we buy and don't eat.

IN THE PISSINGS OF RAIN IN KINVARA

We wandered into a craft shop.
Knowing things the way you do,
—the steadfast sail to my erratic squalls—
you told me the *Wuthering Heights*
score keening from the radio
is based on an old Irish song.

The ring I liked in the cabinet
was a perfect fit. The moulded beaks
like my tattoo, and the coughing corvids
that wheel above our house.

We do not go for superstition.
Prefer the neatly constructed symbolism of ink.
What are constellations if not that?
What other animal could find pictures in the sky?

And yet, you can find a sign
through the drenched windshield
on a motorway pullover, or anywhere,
when the desire is there.

WHISTLE

The lifeguard's whistle blows and
I place my head back in the water,
rippling through the dry follicles
a tingle of submersion
down my neck my elbows.
Like a hot breath wriggling
through the winkle of my ears.

And it's my first time not touching
the bottom, swimming beneath the rope
into the deep end, towards a boy
(of course) who's not yet dead.

My baby is being torn from/to life,
fluorescent light begging me
not to run to it (luckily my legs were frozen).

I am being kissed for the first time.
In a graveyard in the rain (I know, I know).

I'm a broken bird in the enamel bath,
blood up to my elbows. Croaking
my song of *Leave Leave Leave.*

I am seeing the love of my life leaping toward
me through the closing Luas doors (*don't*)
not knowing it will be another five years
before I open my own front door to him (*come in*).

Time is not time it is water,
collapsing
in on itself around a single body
(my body)
falling wilfully, not yet resisting,
giving in
to buoyancy and the present
where the surface
breaks
and the lifeguard's need for air ends
the sound.

ROADKILL: A DRAMA

It was a crime scene made worse
by the early lateness of the hour,
the 4am quiet of club-kicking-out
or airport dashes or this, a careless
cross-country drive, caffeine sick
and wired for a nine o'clock meeting.
The home I left incomplete, my boy
sleeping over with his grandparents.

All to say, I was primed for it: the fear
that lurks around the edges of my days, hides
in children's wardrobes until their parents' patience
is frayed. That keeps the drunk drinking, the priest
praying, and me, writing futile fucking poems.

Yards from our house: a crimson smear
caught by my headlights, black fur mangled
across the broken white line. I U-turn, pull
Cat Dad from sleep like a wailing alarm.
There's no cat at his feet, not unusual
on a dry night like this, mice plentiful
as stars. I bring him, barefoot, to the bend
in the road, wishing minutes passed,
a second set of eyes, might transform
my perception to a carnage-shaped shadow.

Is it him?

> *It's too hard to tell without a head,*

I leave him to stand centurion like
in wait for our cat to not return.

A weepy drive for me, tempted to divert
to my childhood bed, crawl in beside my child,
ask for my mother's reassurance that the dead pet
is not a cause for devastation. The petrol-light

insists. Every closed station pullover a risk.
The petty functions of the world
continue even in the sidelines of horror.
We live to the rhythm of our inconveniences.
Strife unfolds just out of sight., each blind
bend inviting another glass-eyed if-only.

Devastation on the news fails to move me.
I'd run a thousand kittens down myself
to keep my son's beloved cat curled on his bed.

This, what I've tried to keep at bay;
the slap of grief incoming. How to love
what will be snatched away?

The sun does not come up,
but the sky mellows to a pale grey.
Drivers turn off their lights.

I pull into a harbour by the Irish sea.
The Atlantic mist still on my rear windscreen.
A message from Cat Dad pops up:

a picture of our pusheen obliviously happy
on our bed. I sob like a girl: unbridled,
finding all the tears, swallowed, across years,
in favour of more sensible reactions.
For this morning, at least, he's alive,
and none of us are hurting.

PALE BLUE DOT
Extinction is the rule. Survival is the exception.
— *Carl Sagan*

The universe inside a boy. His mother
found all the stars, moons, and worlds
in his telescope mouth.
But mothers do that,
don't they?

In the photograph taken by Voyager 1,
we are no circus in orbit,
but a blue star trapped in sun rays.

A pinprick of light in the dark,
like the zinc firework
of cellular collision, or the spark
of an ultrasound: when a dot
 marks the screen to show life
– where the heart will soon be.

With enough distance we are small.
Krishna could pop Earths like Smarties.

In the right light we are blue fire,
could be mistaken for any one
of a billion gaseous suns
instead of this wet miracle.

With enough distance
you can see
nothing is what it seems.

NOTES

Cirque du Soleil: translates to circus of the sun.

NEBULA

Pilgrimage: The italics in part iv are taken from a gravestone in Haworth Cemetery.

Crescendo: written after Nick Cave's monologue on 'The first time I saw Susie' from the film *20,000 Days on Earth*.

Charlotte Perkins-Gilman: Right-aligned italics are the 'rest cure' by Silas Weir Mitchell. Left-aligned italics are from *The Yellow Wallpaper*.

BIG HOUSE

Character Development: This sequence opens with a quote from George Moore regarding the burning of Moore Hall in 1923, during the Irish Civil War.

A History of Mental Health Care in Five Acts: In addition to the primary sources named below, the writing of this poem was largely informed by *Asylums, Mental Health Care and the Irish 1800-2010* (Irish Academic Press, 2012) edited by Pauline M. Prior.

Irish Lunatic Asylums for the Poor Act 1817: The body of this poem is made from excerpts of the Report from the Select Committee on the Lunatic Poor in Ireland, with minutes of evidence taken before the Committee, 1817. The Act made Ireland the first country in the world to have a national network of publicly funded asylums. The Lunacy Ireland Act formed the basis of mental health care in Ireland from 1821-2015.

The Dangerous Lunatic Act (1838): For the better prevention of crime being committed by the insane: Left aligned text in this poem is taken directly from *1874 Report of the Inspectors of Lunacy.*

Case study: anecdotal evidence from an ordinary provincial mental hospital (1940s/50s): The dialogue in this poem is made up of quotes from Hanna Greally's *birds nest soup.* All quotes are attributed to the characters that speak them in the text.

CARE/COMMUNITY

Care in the Community is a British policy of deinstitutionalisation. This policy influenced Irish deinstitutionalisation. Community based care is still the model used in Ireland today. The specifics and people within this sequence are fictional.

THE ETHICS OF CATS

Neutrality: In 1944 a weather report from Blacksod Lighthouse, Co. Mayo, Ireland, caused Eisenhower to postpone the Normandy landings.

Pale Blue Dot: Krishna is a Hindu deity. The photograph referenced is one of Earth taken by an unmanned space probe from a distance of approximately 6 billion kilometres.

ACKNOWLEDGMENTS

This collection has been a long time coming, and as such there are a lot of people to thank.

My deepest gratitude to all of the following:
Aaron, Stuart, Charley, and all at Broken Sleep Books for their tireless support over the years.

The editors of the publications in which some of these poems first appeared: *Anthropocene, Ambit, Abridged, Banshee, Honest Ulsterman, Icarus, The Irish Times, Poetry Ireland Review, Romance Options (Dedalus Press), Washing Windows Too (Arlen House).*

Special thanks to Bernie Greenan of the Linenhall Arts Centre for commissioning, 'Pulling back the Drapes on a December Morning', and to Dani Gill at The Lighthouse Project for commissioning 'Neutrality'. A video poem of 'Neutrality' was created by Paul Kinsella as part of this commission and can be viewed on YouTube.

For the time, space, and support, thank you to the Arts Council of Ireland, The Rivermill, Cill Rialaig, Listowel Writers Week, Tyrone Guthrie Centre, Words Ireland, the Irish Writers Centre, Druid Theatre, and the Linenhall Arts Centre.

My classmates and the staff of the MA in Writing at University of Galway, where several of these poems began.

Deepest gratitude to Rebecca Goss and Nessa O'Mahoney for their mentorship on an earlier manuscript, parts of which eventually became this book.

The publishers and editors at Doire, Picador, and Mayo Books for their support of my other books, each of which has fed into the next in unpredictable ways.

Les Poétesses: Alicia Byrne Keane, Clíodhna Bhreatnach, Lauren Lawler, Finola Cahill, Fija Callaghan, Róisín Ní Neachtain.

Jessica Traynor, and Liz Quirke, from whom I have learned so much.

Elaine Feeney and Salena Godden for your kind words on this manuscript.

The writers and critics who have taken the time to read and review my work.

The booksellers, producers, festival curators, librarians, volunteers and many unseen roles that go into making a thriving literary scene that means books like this one get an outing.

The many peers and mentors who have had faith, leant sharp eyes and inspiring words.

As always, such love and gratitude to my friends and family, especially mum, for never saying no to a stray kitten.

LAY OUT YOUR UNREST

www.ingramcontent.com/pod-product-compliance
Lightning Source LLC
Chambersburg PA
CBHW032236080426
42735CB00008B/879